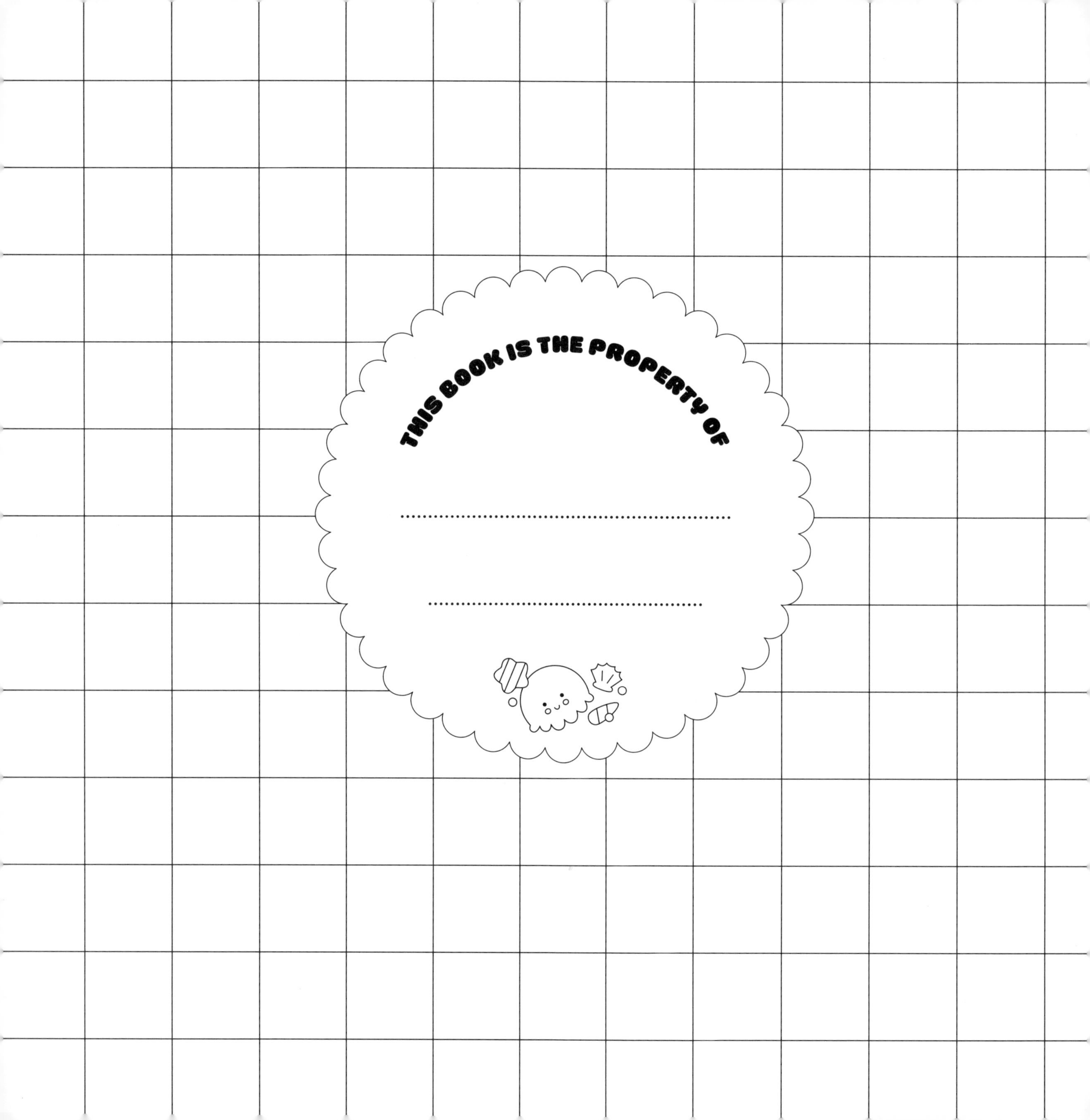
THIS BOOK IS THE PROPERTY OF

Beach Babies Cosy Colouring Fun Kawaii Koala

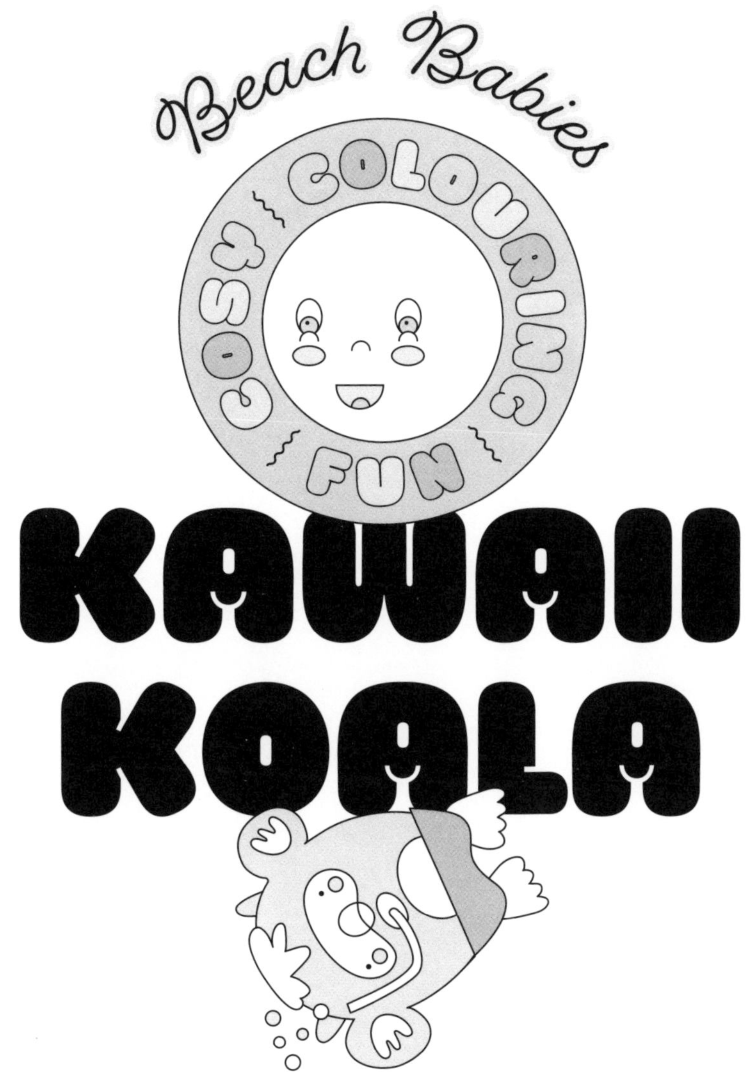

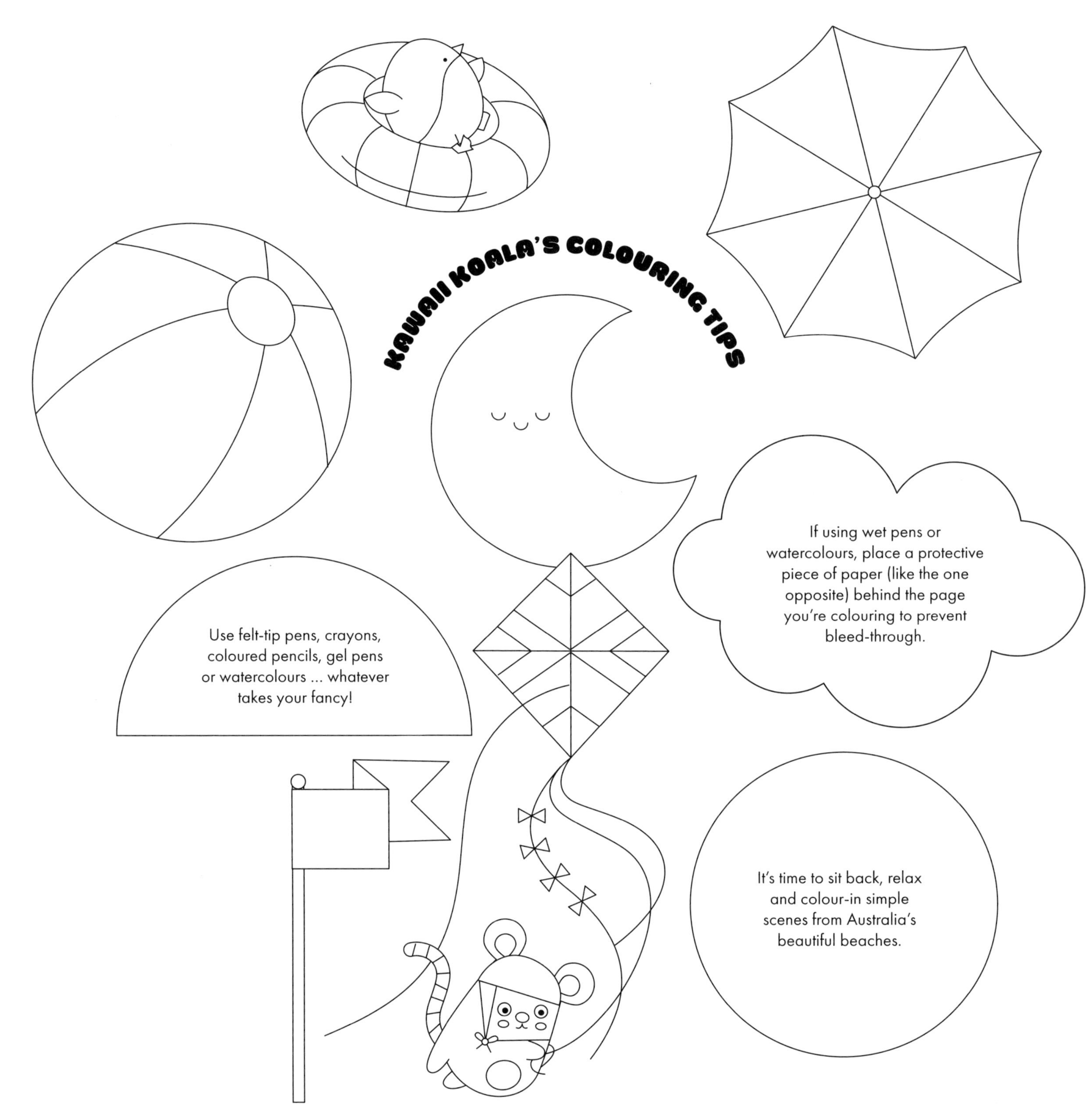
KAWAII KOALA'S COLOURING TIPS
Use felt-tip pens, crayons, coloured pencils, gel pens or watercolours ... whatever takes your fancy!
If using wet pens or watercolours, place a protective piece of paper (like the one opposite) behind the page you're colouring to prevent bleed-through.
It's time to sit back, relax and colour-in simple scenes from Australia's beautiful beaches.

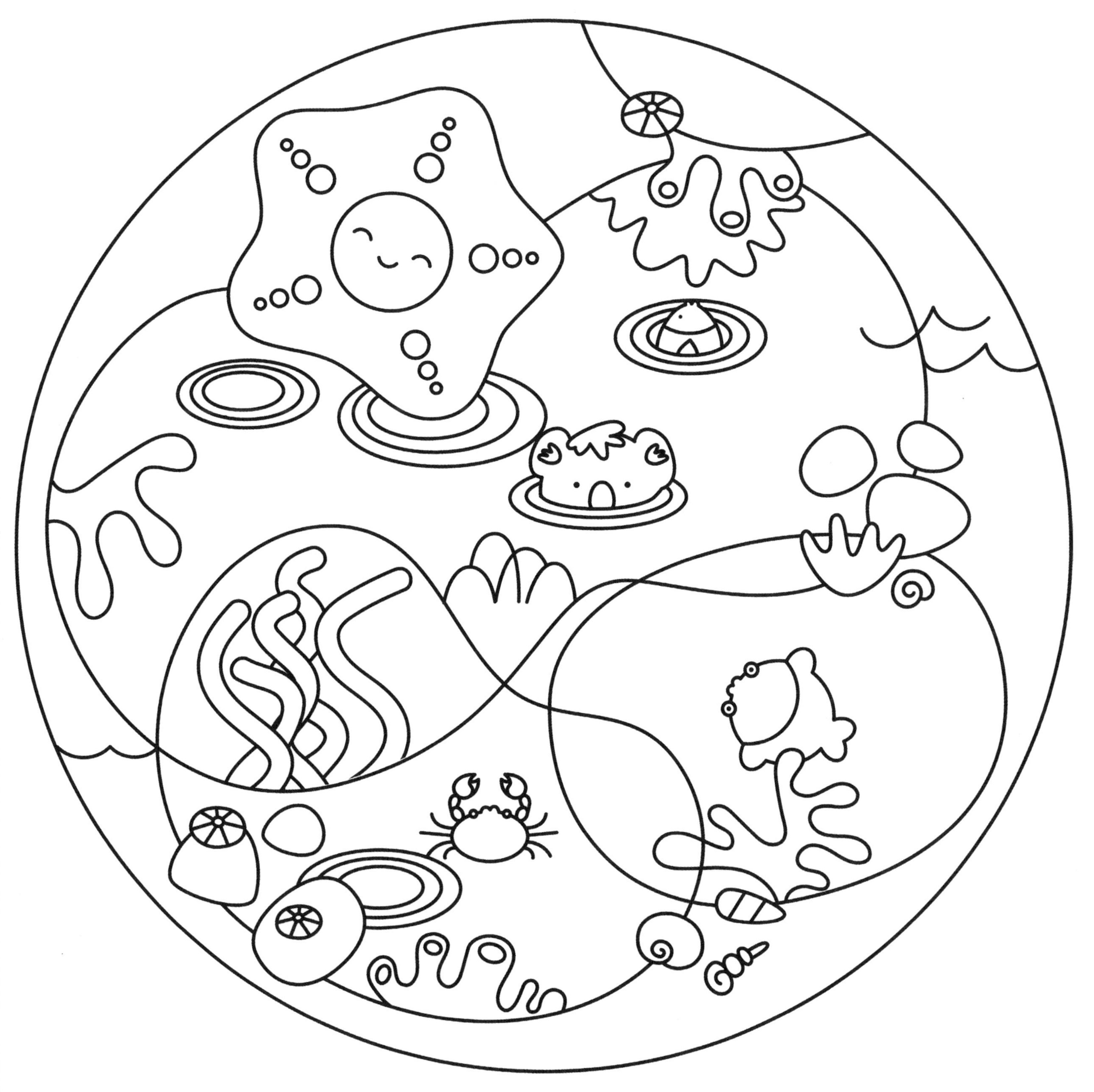

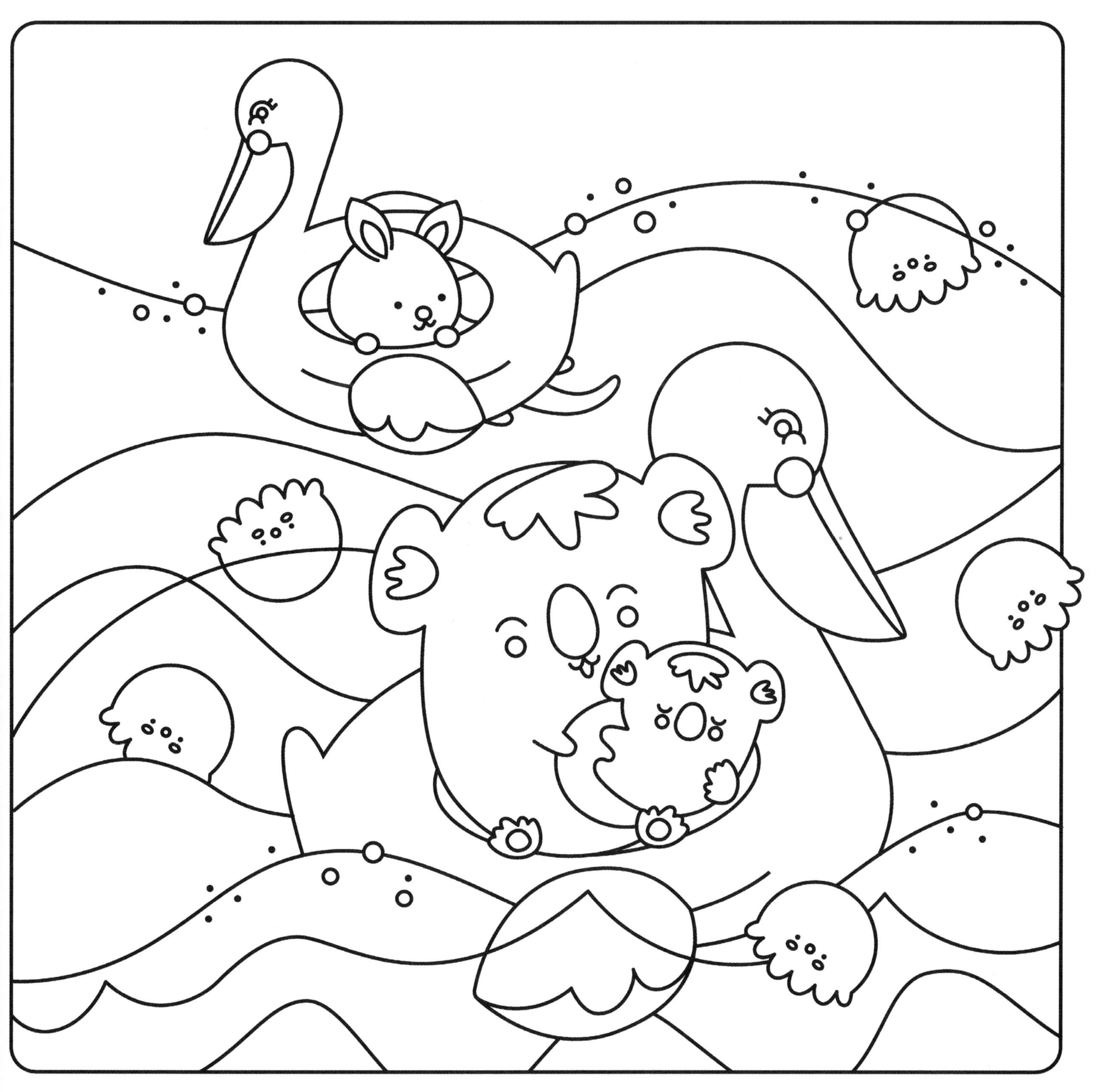

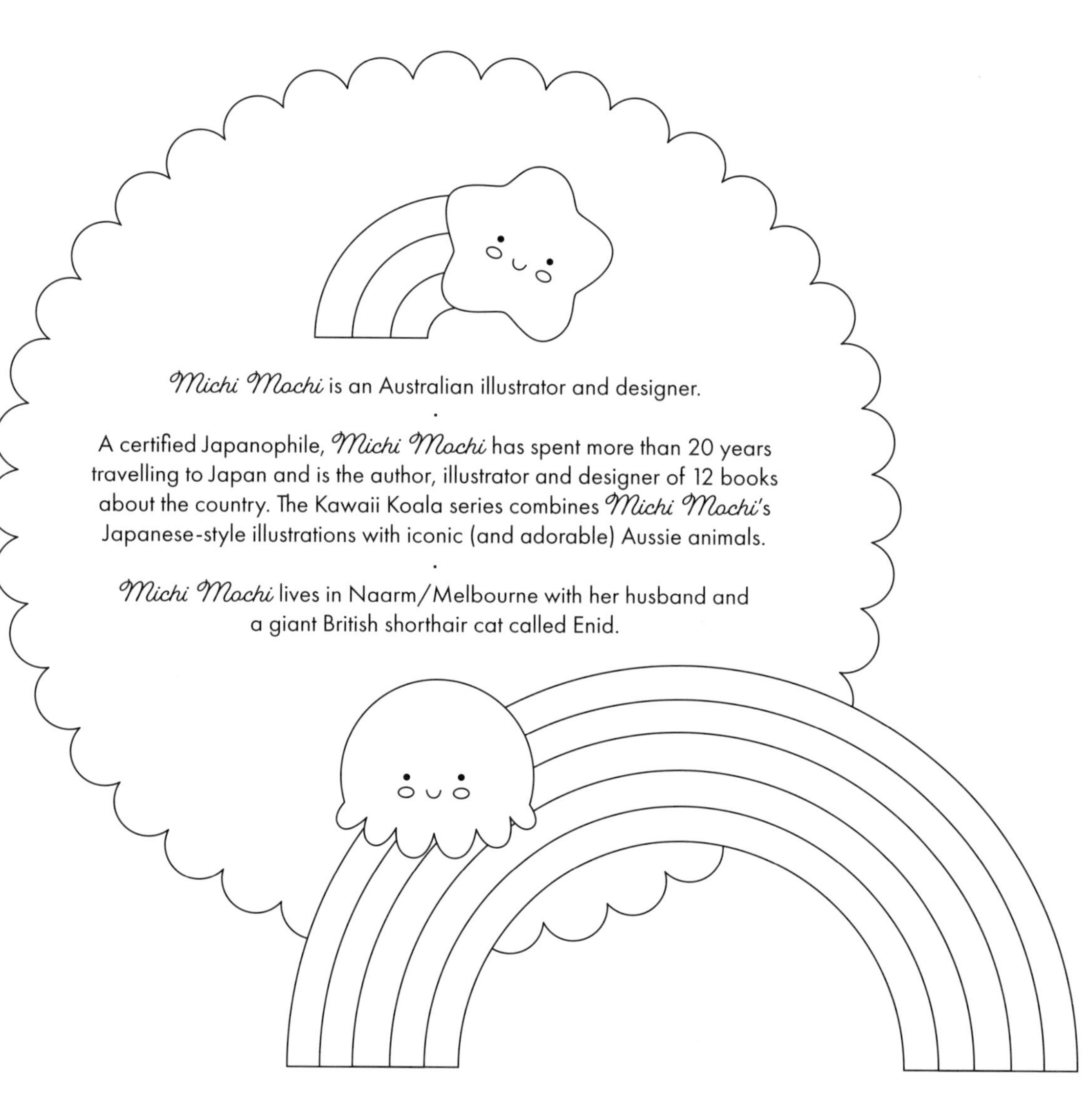

Michi Mochi is an Australian illustrator and designer.

•

A certified Japanophile, *Michi Mochi* has spent more than 20 years travelling to Japan and is the author, illustrator and designer of 12 books about the country. The Kawaii Koala series combines *Michi Mochi*'s Japanese-style illustrations with iconic (and adorable) Aussie animals.

•

Michi Mochi lives in Naarm/Melbourne with her husband and a giant British shorthair cat called Enid.

COLLECT THEM ALL!

Join Kawaii Koala and friends as they enjoy delicious sweets of every stripe in this adorable colouring book for all ages!

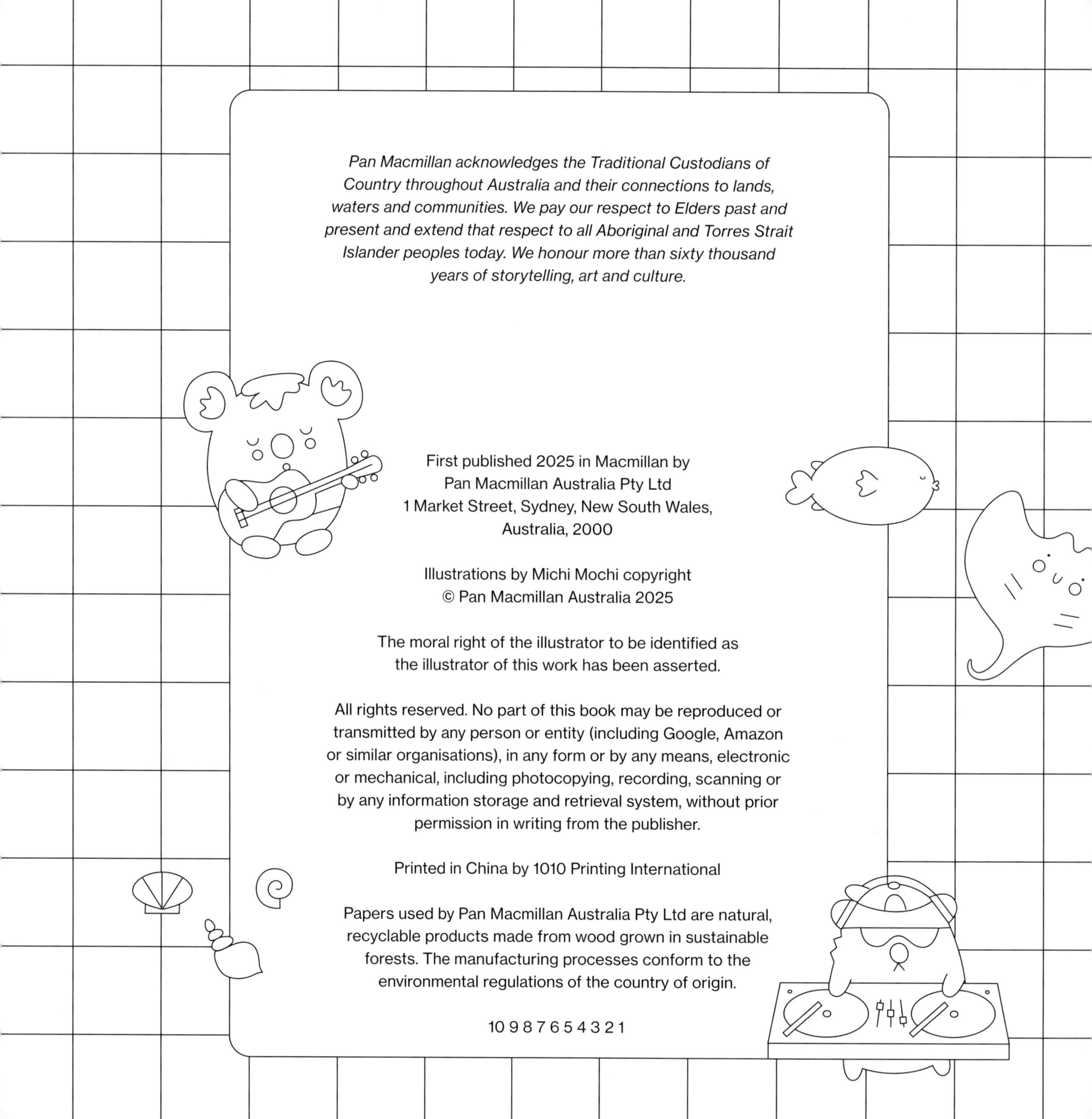

Pan Macmillan acknowledges the Traditional Custodians of Country throughout Australia and their connections to lands, waters and communities. We pay our respect to Elders past and present and extend that respect to all Aboriginal and Torres Strait Islander peoples today. We honour more than sixty thousand years of storytelling, art and culture.

First published 2025 in Macmillan by
Pan Macmillan Australia Pty Ltd
1 Market Street, Sydney, New South Wales,
Australia, 2000

Printed in China by 1010 Printing International

Papers used by Pan Macmillan Australia Pty Ltd are natural, recyclable products made from wood grown in sustainable forests. The manufacturing processes conform to the environmental regulations of the country of origin.

10 9 8 7 6 5 4 3 2 1